MORTAR

MORTAR
SARA MUMOLO

OMNIDAWN PUBLISHING
RICHMOND, CALIFORNIA
2013

Original cover photograph by Arthur Tress
www.arthurtress.com

Book cover and interior design by Cassandra Smith

Offset printed in the United States
by Edwards Brothers Malloy, Ann Arbor, Michigan
on Glatfelter Natures Natural 55# Recycled 30% PCW
Acid Free Archival Quality FSC Certified Paper
with Rainbow FSC Certified Colored End Papers

Cataloguing-in-Publication Data is available from the Library of Congress

Published by Omnidawn Publishing, Richmond, California
www.omnidawn.com   (510) 237-5472   (800) 792-4957
10 9 8 7 6 5 4 3 2 1
ISBN: 978-1-890650-90-2

for Alberto

I.

II. MONEY ON IT

There are blank moments
and I feel sorry for them.

Barbara Guest
"Drawing a Blank"

IN REGARD TO

Trying to avoid a billions-

of-people-type perspective.

Open mouth.

When an index finger slides along a throat.

O. Little blanks.

Bent-orchard-type perspective

I can't afford

the chardonnay California makes.

It is popular for me as a man

to introduce himself

as a woman in this feeling.

When my fingers make an L figure:

a gun on a temple.

Flies issue brief beats,

stomachs taut & iridescent.

On the porch people compare homeless

stories about public shits.

You decide how to palm our change.

Listen Chekhov was a woman.

Wings pause

—flies with their invisible conductors—

then they all tantrum up again, at once.

Bouquets of buildings,

so what if the city wilts around us.

Conversations in and out

black-eyed waves.

By now one of us is angry.

This will want to break the blank

will fail to deposit any widening rings.

Nature-has-come-to-her-senses-type.

Last glass of champagne before your lie,

an empire's ebbing hours,

to ensure we are outside the predicate-act

inform our porch of its impertinence.

Birds curse each other.

Impotence put us in the fear

perspective where I take our blank attitude

& finger-draw a heart

no an apple over your forehead.

A reasonable people in this situation.

Obligatory baiting.

In regard to your wish to trap a world

we are not here, not dead.

THIRD NUDE

We could be nothing but interruptions

        moon-colored snow

if class can belong to a body

you mentioned the moral debt   a mother incurs

when making a parenting error

      (through each entry)

her specter pursues me   its supreme indifferent fiction

  notes between moon & snow

where sunslits graze the bedroom wall

your hand colors a body

it's the health of a nude, not her convention

      (vocabulary is torturous)

to attend her modesty   she's a child-at-play

& we fail to sow Olympia
in my unposed limbs

fragile achievements of uncertainty— pleasure —make her a man

my breasts pulled out of shape because

dank background that maintains our compliance

a breast, a photograph of a breast & the meaning of a breast

yet   beneath my open
arms nothing but shadows

Chaucer used 'aspen' to mean trembling

& I see my hair fail with allowed disorder
                                                    near you

disarm the most comfortable   beliefs

whose earth is not your orphan

what are these people in my life   if not

comes and goers of an outside world

CURRENT

We hear the highway

from the window,

    a sea:

a moneyed wilderness.

In drizzle's colic.

Someone recites this city
as mortar and gulls.

Money is what happens

when one turns to luxury

    for solace.

You believed when they said

the hole will reach China if

Money for the woman discovering

she can never be a sailor.

An artificial product civilization makes
true

When needy I'm French,

shift one word in each cliché.

The ocean builds a hospital

beyond the beams.

MARCH

—lid skipping hardwood.

Revolt you ate

when decency unscrewed.

Dear you   we pretend to be attentive

because we like detail.

I don't recall the bad I did

in a rifle-scope of soot.

First principle of the doctrine of virtue,

my memory and its caterpillar.

Dear I   I want to

live where I travel until I travel

— you say the sun might stain my face.

First principle of the doctrine of right:

A dancer makes a puppet of her

breasts with invisible strings.

Revolt sees

redwoods, and her

nipples cleave your face.

A cleft where

empire heeds:

trucks wasted with goods, trees.

Dear first principle

we should've made you.

Caterpillars bristling,

cocoons recede:

You pretend to be a wave

I try to seal into a jar

LEFT NUDE

Flexible architecture of belonging to someone

we disinter ourselves   as the moon

   what does the moon do

where illusion reigns

    my body is BOOMING

the main ability of a nude is how her figure triumphs

  when earth rehearses her irrelevance

how the city people warned me against

          flung its taut-heart for me

flexed its dim-horizon

   the painter tangles

feeling's color as it brims from pores

    you got to give it to shadows, muddy without relief

these odd-blinking-limbs stymied-drunken-glee

I haul my typical, tapered holes to

      our little convent,

     housing the form of

DECENTRALIZATION OF EASEMENT

Maybe she's as lonely as the rest of us, not comfortable with failure. I step into your voice, its outfit. I watch you wear your voice. You could say I cultivated a face. In your. Makeup. I've packed up all the weather. Men having babies in their paintings. Babies history arrests outside of my museum, which is her museum. I sing into its building, unharvested with echo. Tone on sleeve. She's as lonely as the rest of us, she says. And wears it, disdainfully. I put my cheek on the frame to cool my eyes. You say you're writing *this one as a woman comfortable with failure*. I am breathing this one as a failure comforting her. She writes this uncomfortable movement. This one has a body to zip up. This one is a reel around the baby. A bird's wingspan in a museum, its echo on my tear.

LANDSCAPE WITH A CALM

after Nicolas Poussin

To station presence on day

a nation's shoulder

makes a profession of mute things.

If I am older with morning.

Lake craters

ripples glass:

air's sword

task's shadow

figures meant to fixate

that do once seen

until shadow

until glass.

I transfer money from one imagination to another.

Fuss of us kicking

feet into a chair.

One wants by shape and fray

where valor craters

land stops thinking of you.

I am older this morning.

When shape excuses

and our dog runs off again

making wind seem

wind speed

up and take off the profession

we ask it to admit

until land seems

to heave inside its shadow.

Compare this to a hand

rubbing flecks of old

skin off today.

LOCALE

A whole life doesn't seem enough
to own a body

I'd've breathed as a Riviera

Insurgency
its billowed skin

Made to make
work
how sun fattens around my limbs

What's the verbiage for this   now?

Life seeming
through its hours

I'm not happy in a situation
Only thing admitted here
ring it up

NOT A MASK OF IMMODESTY

In the company of finches
I mail monuments to your
expired home.

What I cup
when we each remain victim to

awkwardness, violence
its bunk rescue from truancy.
Eternally at attention, cowards.

The neighbor's bitch still howls itself to sleep.

Let's get out in the street
share some hypocrisy
with one another. Each time
I aim to scrawl your image
birds—not monuments—rear.
To miss sounds of pencils scratching,
tremble into a school
Each error learns it out.
And rooms, at the address I just sing
so voice has something to listen to.

MIDDLE NUDE

the apparent impossibility of something

                                   first sign of its naturalness

cut out your tongue and make room in there for my heart

how a nude wears

                        her offensive Eve

                        & birch limbs beat windowpanes

even if I could name her   she belongs to disclosure

                                  an unwound leaf,

                                     perishing

physically,   what difference between sound & noise

not imagination or skills   but morale

    it wasn't the land itself

      it was impressions we had before going

in any situation we are involved in coercion

       at least   earth's singing voice

not a leaf of me which does not make itself aware of how

                  worked over it appears

waves fling upcurb   belittled by surface

PHILIP'S GLASS HOUSE

The problem with a heart is that it's too high. I leave a place as if I'd entered it. Air conditioned, here. Invention of, elsewhere. Life so, exhales in glass. Beside preservation, our pulses pull back: hairs reach off my limbs, apropos you. Each of us acting as another copy of the Pantheon. Barely adequate embrace for the space being expressed; lack huddled. Expanded uneven balance of that. It isn't that I miss climbing into a painting—unhung life—wrought by *if I could start it all over, I'd appear earlier.* It's how would we make us when no one admits proportions. Err over earth, veined-neck-view of skies—blue moon. An important shame sheltered up there leaves us to be. When I cool—not everyone inhabits their own pavilion, you did.

NUDES AT DUSK

You hang yourself for the lady

of the house   not its guest

like a guest, I wrought

cash cradle   revises the world

     leitmotif

domestically, incompletely

the courtesan,

       sunshine and shadow show her   shades and sun

cooing tired mystery   solicited privacy

     pale lumps of earth in my pocket where rent

          where your hand should be

so spoke the voice of trade

money's   defensive   dignity

like Gramma swears Elvis lives

how the bourgeoisie believed in Desire

and none of these anxieties are new

desperation, a rope ends it

I believed the pastels sung your voices   up my thigh

new pessimisms?

A redhead   is of a perfect ugliness
bad-luck-baby in Italy hither

the het-up
prostitute, the category

desire or guilt as aspects of each other

I left you   I felt you

necessary twin   myth of social

fear and money tugging pains in the foreground

with my body already lost,
      I'm scared of my mind wandering off

tears of clear/simple

teeth,   soft bones around contention

where a margin of error takes   its place for the system

stakes   the sphinx without her riddle

to call it wise and foolish virgins

MARCH

Ration this real

the whole of it   petitions you

where my fury wraps into a single figure

    it was us the fugue rived to seism.

I am not saying these are odd risks or great displays:

a mist where we   temporarily

The body of a people lies sick…

You can demand

a dove of me, ex post facto.

I am doing this

in my brain

where a human/animal is

melodrama du jour.

Plain way out of fear and monstrosity…

It's banking on a guarantee/

lore we all don't believe   we want

What mattered was

I was practicing life

then land stopped thinking

REPOSE

Frequencies that threaten to

A valleyscape you walked out toward

the street and screamed   staggering

       under reward

Uncanny intensification of alone
means

I understand myself until I heed
privilege

       Events are not
       clear even during   *their occurrence*

Initial pull of the moment ripples   crests

     In a sleep
you invent the weapon I touch you with

THE CALLED BACK WRECK OF THINGS

Our world could not be more up-to-the-minute

I would've put it on mouth as mouth: see sound whole

The clock exhausts its knocking decision

A finger's echo on my chest after the cough chimes down

The stakes, airier than scared to material

Lesion struck moon, impossible to sight or arouse

Sunbathers leisure out, cloaked

My incessant need to tear static without knowing what is

Next the predatory fin floats without floating

We fumble to get our hands in place

Even the victim's stroke, a truck packed with color

I can't help but watch my bodies leap from the chariot

Every seat in the odd upkeep and joust

Move over now for what is obsolete

Shaky hearse of rehearsed preoccupations

A bag's imprint across my breast

Acknowledges that place we flee spoils

What each territory demands

All that crap in my chest

Abides the unattended rotunda at my hips

Veneer over vision baiting

The fooled precession our world is

Or, we enter into identity lugging risks

That we are not reentering it

Snakes are disgusting, I think

About the white flowers as negatives of

The running woman's blank eye-sockets

NUDES NEAR WATER

From the crook of my impatient disease
                              I unfurl

                a blue breathable sky

where the snake is not afraid to sound melodramatic

I'm not that creature anymore
                              mourning her

                own image in an archway

the knife's mood around our edges

                something I say I saw

we're not visible   except as tokens

                generated
                              near context

        balance between hues

                          air apprehends

again   your loud smile

as apprehension etches us

landscapes are something to be

a more humane shake between material and idea

TEMPER ON ITS OWN

A figure of sound measures

The unacceptable way you move

Between viewer and view

Landscape seems invented

This is not cooking music

A full coatrack continues the empty house

I hope you are home when I forget to call

Weeds sieve through mulch

I hate appearing in other people's dreams

A spare key disappears in the pot

Certain aimless alarms

Where plot invents landscape

Three days a week for thirty minutes

I remember why I wake up at night

MONEY ON IT

Now we can know again, even more plainly,
how quickly the world changes.
The land and life are too interrupted
by the indomitable fantasy of extreme violence
…
On the crest of waters we invaded the distance.
Recession will find our shells far: high up in mountains.
It will not be explained how they came there.

William Bronk
"Memorial"

I can't hide you—the rock cried out.

Because the mechanism of surrealism is an activity

not an image—I find embrace in description.

Where a staging of hours counts closer stars

and fails capitalism

—so we may conjoin where air does not—

in San Francisco's parks,

a fog confetti. We unfasten

lids to open brief eyes

across lawns. This is where we ask:

What's the matter with you rock!?

We mouth: P o w e r !

Ducks beak away their feathers,

their plume—in limbo—insults clouds

under this state: how we bankrupt

separation in lieu of—

burning cigarettes through cotton-

money. Breath cleaves

your peering through these holes

when every tree suddenly scents of

cultivation.

Variety is the plastic we make invisible, industry

is everything, even gardenias.

I shop for the end of construct

Where all my actions are.

Progress: our invention likely to commercially exceed,

where real-time grows conceited (extinct). Can we forgo

advancement in favor of shapeliness,

in favor of fields flexed beyond pixelation?

An uneven circus wherever a blank moment and money breed.

Our portmanteau definition is a method of narratology,

our plastic Midwest: a split-screen moral

the starlet strips her wings for

I bite our swarming innards.

Everyone waves around temperature

adults shriek their rap sheets.

A screen I hardly—irresponsibly—write off.

Our flagpoles erect out of pathetic

lawns and no one can remember

when the attacks

day   a local
phenomenon   a burrow
to your pulse   what
forages light

For this image, I cease rotting inside.

Building here, preoccupied with skills,

deer tracks in morning shade.

The men ripping crops, hurling flora…

A method for wearing our desperation objects,

a habit that manages this method,

events nettling.

Genius loci's insider trade says

rainbows are nothing but

constructions of colored paper.

Where amazing is a brief mean of

rememory, not seeds in a sack…

A lantern laments tracks to disease:

Everyone out in the compost at each other's shoulders,

shaking into the product zone.

Bugs are attracted to darkness behind light.

I haul my lungs to the road, unharvested with echo.

We built this city on graves and stone: Oakland nuances.

Measured each step against future campaigns:

each action, a presidential face.

This instance like

a playboy in China eating dog.

Near the freeway: confused concrete employed by brush.

Near its once-a-year pumpkin-patch

I don't seem so abandoned.

Its prairie of fences: MacArthur Maze, sans confidence.

To need this like

shirtless abs on spoiled beaches.

I can remind myself: this is winter; tombs build themselves.

I find the embarrassing object and measure it against your absence.

When we argued about context you really meant images,

and wished everything built off our bodies

into space. Paralysis superimposes

whose capital, sires fig to flag.

Voices slip up words, barely

figured our location by a malaria of seasons:

donottell-donottell-donottell.

In the context of negotiation an offer forms

a fig leaf, if that offer is actually

a ploy to conceal a sinister plan.

Objections we hold

up in front of crowds as leaves:

Royalty unrares reality.

And we transport equivalence from newscast to manufactured-tube.

Unsure how to sign ineligible, do I

our dog star of summer   escorts
air   there   a cavity I built you
when lightning dries   it climbs

I liked the pomp and circumstance.

Stripped along poles,

my demiworld of currency

—cystic eyes—and a soot stage

where militaristic chants desensitize

(the men): It's a broadcast of

ching-chings we imagine

buoys troops through hybrid-stages.

Their uniforms fail us so

we fashion our own audiences

—compelled to enchant—

The safety pin you pierce through your nipple,

and I thought you were brave.

Our outlines inseam

and tailor attractive suffering: bling-bling.

Shock, sign's art.

I am one tendency to demur.

Conflict splays onto circles under slashes:

) contract

) announcement   ) execution

) celebration, stratagem

This search is for motive:

Rings appear as home as home appears pedestrian.

Restive in handicap, we bleed advertisements

Pixels strew the streets, lights

When you mutter: distract our flesh.

I am not a school on fire.

Letters waft—a prettying in flight,

    paper-birds settle the Pacific

    our wave-salute to

Young doves

all have obvious names and role-play:

text-based affairs—skinny-legged jeans

go where money is. Their fiction

saves surrounding mental security

populations and I

feel giant in guilt-sport.

Earth, our unlived life

Cathedral malls litter the beach,

common whores of mankind strung-up

& limp in their windows.

No body can be, except when at a concert,

hands flailing. A communal art

where we fail to examine. Beauty, do you accept

this costume of hairs we fill for gain-pain-gain.

Poles erecting in our master
                    bedroom:
                        DANCE WITH ME!

our cipher-eyes
—impotent antecedents—
do not survive to ration
a real that happens

promise to wear glasses to life's entombment

If math continues, prospects for my life are poor.

Beside droplets of unconfident irony

your smell arrives on the wind.

Gravity and rain

satirize windowpanes.

A law of universal gravitation born from empirical observation

settles nausea between our bodies;

attraction flexes my renaissance-thighs

taut. Sport-of-kings in a celibate-morning

vowing: things are created

Everyone who loves me escapes.

Against a flood of derealization, we near each other in space

Being bottomless as

sound-shards flounder my blouse.

Breath on a neck during sex,

where disappointment sets

its ruffle of light against

a bedroom's sky-stroked walls.

Age of dressing up, shoving

my phallus into fishnets—snap.

This navigation, put money on it—

our mouths around nativity.

My face is a scandal.

Near oblivion youth melts.

Long after Error my inability to peel away,

which is to peel toward you persists:

one never loses the thought of one's capital.

We forget what Names we were.

The palm is human even as I am human.

Sandwich baggie brims with sticks,

I save the bag until I move

a little defense.

Absent aftermath littered

against my complicity

barely in light

bracing and soulful—besieged by touch

Attachment is encouraged among beasts.

Our allowance of careers is the big con.

We hug myself but do not see

your figure disappearing into style

Where is admission to   safety

water advances toward sea

garnishes night
day's labor

menaced between limb & land

I am two tendencies to crack the lion-drum.

As beasts you & I mount globes,

pivot by fore then hinds: jaws and lids seizure

open to gulp the street

—we forget what tour this is—

rid our village of its evil-eye.

I must admit you've been seen

freaking in spring's escapism, revealing

our accursed shares not as the act of

a mechanic changing a tire

but as riding inside the tire itself, wasted.

The village kneading…St. Jerome climbs

out of his pictures and gathers us as pets—

as tigers—the village lives many thorns from here.

I am trying to say without translating.

A male polar bear tore open the neck of a female—

his mephitic fang—they were supposed to mate.

My butcher knife lives in a cupboard above the fridge.

Lions reach through prisons to hug;

Jell-O castles on a merry-go-round.

Our devotion to binoculars:

Parents of 17-year-old Carlos killed by tiger at San Francisco Zoo

say the attack has forever ruined Christmas,

while police investigate if someone helped Tatiana escape.

Tatiana, Siberian, fatally shot by officers

and provoked by Carlos and Co.

is the subject of a life-   scaled sculpture

on Telegraph Hill: Attack survivors collect $900,000.

I am subject to voice.

We think in monochromic color schemes—Blue Period

—a guitar picking out value.

Wally, as a young man in my January class calls him,

knew a thing about the poetry of money. Understanding

equations without tending emotional desperation

rids us of values such as hindsight.

Not cash as a self…

Knifed tree.

Prison-houses where language wires us.

If we are meant, be used, detonate

our chorus, how it bosses plump air into slight math.

look outside   everything is blue
impenetrable-
in-human-distance
voices account   a room

Where I suspend the sight of death

Family wagers where monsoons rock themselves

to sleep & Loretta Lynn brands the-pill.

Tender-loving-care is a twister,

a woman in Arkansas breeding eighteen kids and counting.

Pandemonium buttons up the nation's breast.

> I tie bunny ears around my head with a T.V. cord:

> Loretta mans John Wayne's sinking ship.

> Our screen receives communion.

> I tear out a bible page for you to roll with

> Sorry to bother you in this time of…

> Please think of…

> You'll be in my…

Sixty-two names on a list stroke through

the presidential sea,

a list waiting to move into a tent-village in Pinellas County, Florida.

Our world-method for measuring distance

saunters off.

…sort-of-way economy and we move over roads.

I know to put on cooking music by Point Defiance ferry bells.

Spend three hours to cross the Sound.

Waiting for someone to see our bodies, we push

past masses for one particular recognition.

What we call Rush Hour is a skill

and its product is that nothing feels rushed:

running through water.

I never learn the language made for us all.

Everyone's face strapped on by collars of incognito.

How would we sign when altered by slips in coordinates…

I'm crying in an airport food court where

we construct approval of my emotional desperation,

which occurs from lack of exchange. Maybe I've heard

death news, the father. Peering

into this court: Here, a table

because my hand sleeps on it.

Action. Not narrative

and a napkin crumpled beyond my abilities.

—it skids. Poussin's *Landscape with a Man Killed by Snake* erects

around me—3-D resembles our world now,

only more stylish. What voice

we allow out of the house and how we leak inside it.

dark simply
gloom still   cast by hill
obscene knowing

A parapet of clouds I recall.

A moon of hurt, your line I repeat

to myself, makes me

love in an unexchangeable way.

Idiom of air where I leave English to retire.

Several pieces of light from fingers:

we float out graves and fall back in the same way.

I succumb to the alien & wholly uncongenial.

Not retired heroines, childhood irrigates

no-one-will-come-for-us.

Deafness and infancy-shrapnel

—a hiss inside me—

Money's cavity & cannon,

I cannot find age's script by looking:

California's fire season resembles our treason.

Not everyone will live there; we did.

I am not negotiating earth's elegy.

Our costume is that we keep connected,

terrorist fist-bump…

terra suffused…

Slight away male costumes—

A new way to deliver this to you?

—occupation of building me. A dream:

You're walking right off Federal Hall steps,

      plummeting awake.

Not a metonym, Wall Street's sign is posted

where Melville's lawyer struggles to reason

that which is unreasonable. Shouldered

beyond to feel something real.

Put on the sumptuous monuments one face at a time.

We're not able to fail the direction of war clouds, spatially.

And in temporal crooks we wake

where here-there is a statue off the freeway,

where graffiti fashions wind,

tattoos leaves into metronomes of text.

      —I mean we don't hear

as if exchange is other than bazaars or blasts.

In battle I'm your empty-

socketed spectator

whose blinks open one moment

then trade it—hello—there are two-faces who live

unconcealed on my skull. Flesh scrunches.

Rolling over onto backs, we're conflict's mascot.

ACKNOWLEDGMENTS

Thank you to the editors of the following journals where poems in this manuscript previously appeared: *1913: a journal of forms*; *Action Yes*; *Coconut*; *comma, poetry*; *Eleven Eleven*; *Lana Turner*; *The Offending Adam*; *Real Poetik*; *West Wind Review*; *The Volta*; and *Volt*. A few of the poems in the manuscript appeared in various forms in the chapbook *March* published by Cannibal Books in 2011.

Thank you to and for my teachers, readers, and friends for supporting this collection of poems: Clay Banes, Norma Cole, Jane Gregory, Graham Foust, Gillian Hamel, Ken Keegan, Amanda LaBerge, Pablo Lopez, Brenda Hillman, Geoffrey G. O'Brien, Joseph Massey, Richard Meier, Rusty Morrison, Vicente Peñuela, Chris Sindt, Cassandra Smith, Brian Teare, and Sharon Zetter.

Gratitude to my family for supporting my imaginative life: Lila Mumolo, Nikki Mumolo, and Jacob Richardson. Thank you to my partner, Alberto Madueño, and our soon-to-arrive baby, who should be in the world by the time this book is published.

Thank you to the Saint Mary's College of CA community for providing me with lifelong friends from my days as a graduate student to my current position as the MFA Program Manager. Thank you for fostering a community where both a practical and imaginative life can flourish.

Finally, thank you to everyone at Omnidawn for all your work and vigor making beautiful books every season. Thank you especially to Rusty Morrison and Ken Keegan who brought this book into the world, and to Cassandra Smith for the design. They make everyone at Omnidawn feel like family, and I'm thrilled to be a part of that family.

Sara Mumolo is the Program Manager for the MFA Program in Creative Writing at Saint Mary's College of California, where she also received her MFA in creative writing. She is the co-editor of the chapbook series *Calaveras*. She created the Studio One Reading Series in Oakland, California, and was its curator from 2008 to 2012. Cannibal Books published her chapbook, *March*, in 2011. Her poems have appeared in *1913: a journal of forms*, *Action Yes*, *Coconut*, *Eleven Eleven*, *Lana Turner*, *The Offending Adam*, *Real Poetik*, *Typo*, *The Volta*, and *Volt*, among others. She lives in Oakland, California.

Mortar
by Sara Mumolo

Cover text set in Gill Sans Std and Hypatia Sans Pro.
Interior text set in Adobe Garamond Pro and Perpetua Titling MT.

Original cover photograph by Arthur Tress
www.arthurtress.com

Cover and interior design by Cassandra Smith

Omnidawn Publishing
Richmond, California
2013

Rusty Morrison & Ken Keegan, Senior Editors & Publishers
Cassandra Smith, Poetry Editor & Book Designer
Gillian Hamel, Poetry Editor & OmniVerse Managing Editor
Sara Mumolo, Poetry Editor
Peter Burghardt, Poetry Editor & Book Designer
Turner Canty, Poetry Editor
Liza Flum, Poetry Editor & Social Media
Sharon Osmond, Poetry Editor & Bookstore Outreach
Juliana Paslay, Fiction Editor & Bookstore Outreach Manager
Gail Aronson, Fiction Editor
RJ Ingram, Social Media
Pepper Luboff, Feature Writer
Craig Santos Perez, Media Consultant